Original title:
Rhymes in the Rift

Copyright © 2025 Creative Arts Management OÜ
All rights reserved.

Author: Julian Carmichael
ISBN HARDBACK: 978-1-80567-826-7
ISBN PAPERBACK: 978-1-80567-947-9

Melodies Beneath the Surface

In the pond a frog does croak,
Its bassy notes like a joke.
The fish swim by, roll their eyes,
While the snail just sighs and tries.

A turtle hums a silly tune,
Underneath the light of the moon.
With bubbles popping, they all laugh,
A chorus formed of the pond's staff.

Chords from the Chasm

In a canyon deep, a cat does sing,
Alping with echo—a curious thing.
A raccoon joins with a clatter and clank,
While a coyote wails and thanks!

The stones below tap, clap in delight,
As shadows dance through the moonlight.
"Oh, what a band!" the owl hoots loud,
As laughter floats over the crowd.

Reflections of Dissonance

A goat on a hill sings flat as can be,
While cows join in harmony, just to be free.
The hens are clucking a cacophony bright,
In a barn where the echoes are pure delight.

A pig tries to whistle, it sounds like a breeze,
All the critters can't help but giggle with ease.
As they create noise, a symphony wild,
In this raucous barn, no one's riled.

Lyrics in the Limbo

In the limbo where shadows twist,
A fox with a hat can't resist.
He dances around with a comical flair,
While ducks just quack, with feathers in the air.

The shadows chuckle, they spin with grace,
As each silly step finds its place.
A world made of giggles, so delightfully bright,
In this playful limbo, all feels just right.

Symphonies of Solace

In a world full of chatter, cats dance on toes,
While gardeners giggle at their wayward hose.
Balloons in the sky, with a whimsical sway,
Chasing a butterfly who's lost his way.

Llamas in pajamas, they strut with such flair,
Tripping on rainbows without a care.
Bananas in pockets, a slippery plight,
Sliding down rainbows, oh, what a sight!

The moon wears a hat, with a grin wide and bright,
Juggling with stars, in the deep of the night.
Frogs play the banjo on lily pad seats,
Paddleboat whales keep the rhythm with beats.

So join in the laughter, let joy be the key,
Where whimsy and wonder unite with glee.
For life's but a circus, a show full of cheer,
Embrace all the oddities, nothing to fear!

Waves from the Wilderness

Amidst the tall woods, a squirrel spins tales,
Of acorns and treasure hunts, giggling snails.
Frolicking foxes in boots made of lace,
Sipping on nectar, a sweet little grace.

Pinecones are hats for the wise old owl,
Who hoots with delight, and starts to howl.
The rabbits in coats are throwing a bash,
While a turtle in shades plays the ukulele flash.

Dancing in meadows, the daisies take flight,
Tickling the grass in a jovial sight.
As fish in the brook wear glasses and read,
The laughter of nature plants a bright seed.

So drift with the waves, let the humor unfold,
In a realm where silliness never grows old.
From the canopy whispers to the creek's gentle lap,
Find joy in the wild, let your heart take a nap!

Sonnet of the Solitude

In a room so empty, a sock takes flight,
The goldfish stares, it knows of my plight.
I ask it for wisdom, it bubbles back,
Stuck in a bowl, it swims with no knack.

My chair, a companion, creaks with a sigh,
It knows all my secrets, my dreams that defy.
Together we ponder, of cheese and of jokes,
While the clock on the wall just puffs like a folks.

Rifts of Resonance

In the middle of nowhere, I play with a broom,
It waltzes around me, it brightens the gloom.
The cat gives a chuckle, or so it appears,
As I tango with dust, while it sneezes in cheers.

My kitchen's a circus, a salad in flight,
A tomato just leaped, oh what a delight!
The blender joins in with its whirring refrain,
While I dance with my snacks, and I'll never complain.

Ballads from the Beyond

A toaster is singing, a breadroll in hand,
As I tap my feet to the warm breakfast band.
The coffee pot giggles, a wake-up delight,
Whisking me softly into morning's bright light.

And the sugar, it dances, a sweet little twirl,
While my pancakes slide down for a syrupy whirl.
In this kitchen of joy, oh, what a surprise,
Even the butter joins in with a rise!

Voices from the Vortex

Up in the attic, the dust bunnies chat,
While I'm down below, with a curious cat.
The vacuum cleaner hums, a bassline it gives,
As I pull out old outfits from when I was five.

The ghosts of my childhood, they giggle and sway,
At the sight of my fashion from back in the day.
Twirl with a tutu, oh what a sight,
In this old dusty den, where laughter takes flight.

Dreamscapes of Duality

In a land where socks all dance,
A shoe took up a bold romance.
The spoon began to spin around,
While forks just laughed and made a sound.

Beneath the sun, the teacups sing,
As penguins sport their finest bling.
A cat in stripes begins to skip,
While dogs all twirl and do a flip.

The clouds play games of hide and seek,
While elephants ride on a creek.
The trees wear hats, oh what a sight,
As stars emerge to join the night.

Meditations on the Divide

A squirrel spoke in rhymes about,
The cheese that caused a giant pout.
With laughter bouncing off the walls,
The moon tried dancing at the stalls.

A turtle broke the speed record,
While laughing, said, "I love the herd!"
The palm trees tossed their coconuts,
At jokers in bright feathered cuts.

Behind the clouds, a lion roared,
As all the jesters drew a board.
With every tickle on the breeze,
The flowers chuckled with such ease.

Imagery from the Interlude

Two hats were chatting on a chair,
While coats discussed their favorite hair.
The tables wobbled, chairs applauded,
As wild cat's yarn was quickly knotted.

A parrot squawked, "I told a joke!"
The wall replied, "You're such a bloke!"
In corners where the teacups dwell,
A coffee pot started to tell.

The cupcakes rolled in patterned dress,
While cookies played a card game mess.
The jam in jars did stand and twirl,
In this mad, sweet, wobbly world.

Contrapuntal Crossroads

At the fork where toasters fight,
One burnt a crumpet out of spite.
The kettle whistled, 'What a show!'
While jellybeans began to flow.

The pizza slice and burger danced,
Making everyone quite entranced.
But all the fries just rolled their eyes,
As carrots tried to win the prize.

A pickle played a ukulele,
With apples spinning, acting crazy.
At crossroads where the laughter swells,
The rhythm of the kitchen bells.

Syllables in the Abyss

In the deep, words wiggle and dance,
Sentences stumble, a curious chance.
Puns dive down, with water so cool,
Grammar's a fish, just playing the fool.

Submerged in a sea of quirky delight,
Can laughter float up, if we get it right?
With buoyant puns swimming near the sand,
We'll catch a big laugh with a playful hand.

Verses of the Void

In the void, a word takes flight,
It tickles the silence, oh what a sight!
A joke gets lost in a cosmic spin,
But echoes of giggles pull it back in.

Space ticks in rhythms both strange and bright,
Pantomime verses soar high with delight.
With mischief abounding in every gap,
The cosmos erupts—what a funny trap!

Harmonies of Broken Bridges

A bridge made of giggles, it sways in the breeze,
Each step sends a chuckle, it's sure to appease.
With laughter as nails, and joy for the wood,
It's wobbly, yes, but oh so good!

Across the divide, where silence should reign,
The sound of a pun jumps right off the plain.
With each little wobble and each funny slip,
We sway to the rhythm, with a giggling quip.

Stanzas in the Shadows

In shadows of giggles, the stanzas collide,
With whispers of humor that tickle and slide.
They hide and they seek in a play full of cheer,
A mystery wrapped in a pun yet unclear.

With shadows that chuckle and stanzas that smile,
We dance in the dusk, let's stay for a while.
For every odd phrase is a spark to ignite,
A laughter-filled journey, oh what a delight!

Cadences of the Unknown

In a land where socks dance solo,
And spoons hold court with the jello,
A cat declares it's time to play,
Why chase the night when we can sway?

A plant insists it tells the news,
While chairs complain that they're misused,
The fridge hums tunes of summer breeze,
And all the ants are on the tease.

The clock strikes twelve without a sound,
While puddles giggle on the ground,
A mushroom wears a tiny hat,
As turtles throw a funky spat.

With laughter echoing far and wide,
In this bizarre fun-fair we glide,
Each twist and turn brings giggles bright,
In the dance of day and night.

Poetry of Fractured Paths

A toaster mutters jokes at dawn,
While fish in suits are up for lawn,
The rabbit hops in polka dots,
In this mad world, they tie their knots.

Sidewalks bend under the weight,
Of grasshoppers who love to skate,
Streetlights wink in playful jest,
While squirrels pretend they are the best.

A feather floats just out of reach,
While clouds above aim to impeach,
A bookworm spins a yarn so tall,
That even ants begin to crawl.

In the circus of the common fate,
We gather 'round and celebrate,
Each stumble leads to laughter grand,
In this twisted, funny land.

Notes from the Nether

A shadow sings in tuneful glee,
While brooms take flight, so wild and free,
Ghostly whispers chase the moon,
To the beat of a funky tune.

Potatoes prance in shiny shoes,
With veggies sharing gossip news,
A pumpkin dressed in vibrant shades,
Tells tales of fun that never fades.

The lantern flies, they do a dance,
While socks lost in the cosmic trance,
With silly hats and playful cheer,
They toast to life and pass the beer.

In the nether, jesters reign supreme,
Crafting laughter from a dream,
With silly songs and merry glee,
This realm's the wildest place to be.

Tales from the Edge

On the edge where giggles thrive,
A crab waltz brings a joyful jive,
While roller skates on broccoli,
Invite the bees to dance with glee.

The moons discuss their awkward spins,
While ants debate their favorite bins,
A cupcake floats with icing high,
And dares the fruit flies to the sky.

Beneath the stars, the marshmallows feast,
As raccoons claim they've caught a beast,
A rubber duck leads all the fun,
While clocks with wings begin to run.

From the edge of strangeness we peek,
Into a world that loves to speak,
With laughter bursting, joy takes flight,
In the tales spun from sheer delight.

Echoing Beyond the Edge

In a village where chickens play,
The cows dance into the fray.
Frogs sing operas on the rise,
While goats ponder in disguise.

The sky is split with jokes so bright,
As squirrels juggle 'til the night.
A rabbit hopscotches in glee,
Hopping over a drowsy bee.

Pigs wear hats and sashay around,
Making music without a sound.
A sheep conducts the whole parade,
To a beat that cannot fade.

The border is just a laughing line,
Where laughter grows on every vine.
So join the fun, don't take a rift,
Embrace the strange, that's the gift!

Odes to the Outskirts

At the edge where odd meets fun,
A bull plays chess with a runny bun.
The moon dips down to catch a tease,
While owls crack jokes from the trees.

A picnic spread with pies that hum,
As ants march by in a crazy drum.
The sun throws shade on playful games,
Where everyone is known by names!

Goats in capes leap over logs,
Making friends with passing dogs.
A dance-off breaks out by the creek,
Where turtles twist and chickens squeak.

In this land of snippets and quirks,
Laughter blooms where chaos lurks.
So tip your hats and join the tune,
In this wacky world beneath the moon.

Songs of the Separated

A cat serenades a lonely shoe,
While mice debate what cheese is true.
The clock now a disco ball,
Tick-tocks inviting one and all.

A fence that leans to tell a tale,
Of a snail daring to set sail.
Frogs in tuxedos croon each night,
Swapping wishes and delight.

Beneath the stars, they hold a feast,
Inviting every furry beast.
The whispers swirl on breezes tight,
As fireflies flash in sheer delight.

In this space where odd meets clear,
Laughter rings out, loud and near.
So gather close and lend an ear,
To songs that celebrate the cheer.

Cadenced Cracks

In the pavement where cracks make jokes,
A squirrel shares puns with the folks.
The benches giggle beneath the sun,
While a dancing leaf has a bit of fun.

At the corner, a lamp post stands,
Holding secrets from distant lands.
Blurred lines between silly and real,
As shadows toss bananas to peel.

Down by the park, a kite takes flight,
Dancing with clouds in pure delight.
A dog chases after a wayward cat,
Both tangled in a comedy spat.

So step on the cracks, don't fear the break,
Each stumble, a laugh, for goodness' sake.
In this world, every quirk's a boon,
Embrace the fun beneath the moon.

Fables of Forgotten Bridges

There once was a bridge made of cheese,
A mouse had a party, oh what a tease.
The cars took a bite, and the drivers did squeak,
As the bridge melted down in its gooey peak.

A turtle once tried to cross it at night,
With a lantern that flickered, oh what a sight.
He slipped on a cracker and fell with a splash,
Left the mice all in stitches, they giggled and gashed.

The bridge held the laughter, the joy, and the glee,
With a fashion show hosted by quirky old Bee.
The insects wore outfits of twigs, leaves, and fluff,
While the cheese bridge looked on, saying, "This is enough!"

But soon the cheese vanished, the party all fizzed,
And the mouse looked around, saying, "What have we missed?"
With no bridge for dancing, they hid in the cracks,
And promised next time they'd wear less of the snacks.

Tones of Twilight

The moon wore a hat made of purple silk,
While crickets chirped songs like cups full of milk.
A cat in a bow tie danced on the street,
As the stars twinkled back with a flick of their feet.

A frog wearing glasses sang karaoke,
While the fireflies joined in, feeling quite pokey.
They croaked such odd tunes, oh what a delight,
That even the owls hooted loud with delight.

Bats joined the party, all swinging so low,
They dipped and they dived in a flash of a show.
Their wings were like capes, flowing bold in the night,
As shadows danced freely, twirling with fright.

In the end, all the critters lay down with a cheer,
Under the blanket of stars, feeling clear.
They laughed and they snored until dawn broke the fun,
Then promised to meet when the next day is done.

Ballads Bound by Distance

A penguin took flight on a bright paper plane,
Waving to seals while it danced in the rain.
The ocean was restless, but he felt quite fine,
As the fish cheered him on with a chorus divine.

A lion on land wrote a letter so grand,
Asked the penguin to join him on warm sandy strand.
With a pen made of whiskers, he scribbled with flair,
"I'll share my sunbathing, bring your own chair!"

A sloth read the mail, nearly fell from a tree,
"Deliver it fast!" He said, "Hurry, you see!"
But the turtle was busy with snacks, oh what glee,
Mounting a feast of old leaves, just wait and see.

In the end, the penguin set sail with a wish,
To meet up with friends and devour a dish.
But little did he know, that the lion snoozed,
And they still have to wait for the fast-food cruise!

Rhythms from the Rifted Realm

In a realm where the goats wore pajamas and hats,
They danced to the beats made by two clever cats.
With tambourines jingling and laughter so loud,
The goats leaped around, feeling silly and proud.

A dog in a tutu twirled 'round the floor,
While the cats sang along, what a raucous uproar!
They slid on the tiles, then slipped on the mats,
As the goats joined in, making piratey spats.

A hedgehog, quite suave, joined in with the flow,
With a top hat and cane, he put on quite a show.
"Step right up, everyone! Come see our dance!"
With a wink and a twirl, he gave fate a chance.

As the sun began to set on their giggly delight,
They partied in shadows, till stars filled the night.
With echoes of laughter, they bid each adieu,
And swore that tomorrow they'd do it anew!

Harmonies in the Hollow

In a place where giggles hide,
Laughter echoes, can't abide.
Silly birds with hats so bright,
Dance around in pure delight.

Wobbling bunnies play a tune,
Juggling carrots, oh, so soon!
Moonbeams tickle the grass below,
As playful shadows put on a show.

A frog in shades croaks a rhyme,
Counting stars, it's nearly time.
With a wink, he leaps up high,
Lands in pie—you should just try!

In this hollow, laughter's gold,
Tales of silliness unfold.
Join the dance, don't just sit,
Life's a stage where chuckles fit.

Balancing on the Brink

On the edge of silly jokes,
Wobbly stands of dancing folks.
Juggling pies and flying hats,
Who knew clowns could be such brats?

A cat on stilts, oh what a sight!
Chasing tails in pure delight.
Slips and slides, a wild spree,
Balance lost on the big, bright tree.

Whispers loud as gaffes abound,
Laughter springs from splatters round.
Balancing on a funky rhyme,
Every tumble, a perfect crime!

With each slip, the crowd erupts,
Facial pies and paint corrupts.
Standups fumble, one by one,
In this fun, we all have won.

Stanzas from the Shadows

In the dark where shadows play,
Scribbled words in disarray.
Limericks flicker, dance and prance,
Whispers funny, take a chance.

Ghosts of humor float about,
With silly jokes, they twist and shout.
Each stanza flutters, softly falls,
Echo in those shadowed halls.

A wacky tune from somewhere near,
Bouncing off each ancient sphere.
Riddles leap from nook to nook,
Punny tales in every book.

As laughter wraps the silent night,
Forget your worries, hold on tight.
In these dark, forgotten places,
Joy unfurls, in funny embraces.

Unraveled Lines of Divergence

Lines confused, a twisted fate,
Unraveled tales that momentate.
Sneaky squirrels with acorn plans,
Plot to dance with happy fans.

Wobbling words on a curvy road,
Splitting paths, like heavy load.
Every twist a chuckle brings,
Swirling songs on fluttering wings.

Jokes collide like bumper cars,
Crashing laughter, rising stars.
What a sight, this comic clash,
Each misstep a funny splash!

In this mess, a joy derived,
Each turned line becomes alive.
Divergence leads to goofy times,
So gather round for silly rhymes!

Vibrations of the Unseen

In shadows where the giggles bloom,
A tomato jokes with a dancing broom.
They spin and sway in a lunchtime spree,
Pretending to sip on imaginary tea.

The cat wears a hat, a fine little sight,
Reciting itself in the soft moonlight.
It stumbles and tumbles, a jester's sweet glee,
Chasing the mouse who's as quick as can be.

With whispers of laughter that float in the air,
The puppy trips over its own fluffy hair.
There's a tree who's aging, but still tells a joke,
While squirrels roll around in a leafy cloak.

Oh, the world's full of wiggles and giggles galore,
With stories of carrots and much, much more.
So join in the jest, let your spirit take flight,
In this carnival universe, everything feels right.

Lines Between the Lost

A shoe found a hat in the middle of a street,
They argued politely as friends often meet.
"Your laces are tangled!" the hat did exclaim,
While the shoe just danced, forever unashamed.

A squirrel with glasses read books upside down,
While pigeons wore bowties and waltzed through the town.
In the corners of sidewalks where puddles reside,
Laughed the worm with a top hat, oh what a ride!

The moon winked at clouds that did float and did swirl,
While stars played hopscotch with the night as their girl.
Each critter and creature, in whimsical glee,
Shared secrets of laughter for everyone to see.

In the tapestry woven of chuckles and cheer,
Things lost now are treasures, so vibrant and near.
Amongst all the quirks, life's humor stands tall,
Where even the awkward can shine and enthrall.

Songs of the Uncharted

There's a lighthouse that sings to the ships out at sea,
With a voice like a banshee, so wild and so free.
Its beams write sonnets on waves as they pass,
While seagulls join in, putting sails made of glass.

A crab in a tuxedo proposes a dance,
Inviting the fish for a whimsical chance.
The octopus juggles while making a stew,
Crafting meals of noodles that tickle the blue.

With bubbles that giggle and tickle the tide,
The concert goes on with no place left to hide.
Mermaids are laughing, their tails all askew,
As they tap out a rhythm on drums made of dew.

Here in the waters where laughter is spun,
Everything's funny, and nothing's undone.
So follow the melody wherever it goes,
In the music of mischief, hilarity flows.

Cadence of the Cleft

Up a hill where the snickers align,
A goat with a flute hits a note so divine.
It toots and it moans, with a rhythm to spare,
While geese in a circle dance without a care.

The flowers giggle in colors so bright,
Every petal a punchline, a source of delight.
With bees doing ballet in pollen-filled streams,
They whisper sweet secrets in sunshine and dreams.

Down by the creek where the frogs entertain,
Wearing tiny bowler hats, they sing in the rain.
The fish throw confetti; it sparkles in flight,
As laughter erupts from the softening night.

In this place where the funny runs wild and free,
Every shadow and echo becomes a decree.
So tiptoe with joy, let your spirit ascend,
For in every small moment, there's fun without end.

Echoes of Dissonance

A cat in a hat sat on a mat,
Chasing its tail, what do you think of that?
The dog next door played the trombone loud,
While the fish in the tank had a chat with a crowd.

The bird in the tree sung in perfect tune,
But slipped on a branch and flew to the moon.
With laughter so loud, it broke the day,
We all laughed together, hip-hip-hooray!

Verses in the Divide

Two ants danced on a picnic crust,
Spinning and twirling, oh what a must!
A bee in the flower giggled with glee,
While pollen tickled the nose of a flea.

A frog in a bog croaked jokes to the crowd,
Jumping and leaping, feeling quite proud.
The sun started smiling, brightening the day,
As nature joined in the playful ballet.

Whispers Across the Abyss

A turtle took off in a race with a hare,
But fell on its back and couldn't find air.
The hare stopped to laugh, 'You're quite the slowpoke!'
While the crow in the sky dropped a witty joke.

The wind tried to whisper, but just blew through,
Tickling the grass and the wildflowers too.
With giggles and snorts, the whole world joined in,
Creating a symphony, where fun would begin.

Chords of the Chasm

A jester once tripped on a big pair of shoes,
Landed in popcorn, shouting, "I'll choose!"
The crowd erupted in fits of delight,
As he juggled some apples and danced with a kite.

Nearby, a goat played a fiddle so sweet,
Bouncing to tunes that fun-loving feet.
With laughter as music, the night turned to day,
Where silliness ruled in the silliest way.

Echoes of the Expanse

In the vastness where echoes play,
A cat sings tunes in a playful way.
Socks on its paws, it starts to prance,
Moonlit dance, oh what a chance!

A pickle jar joins in the fun,
Bouncing around like it's on a run.
With giggles and hiccups, they hop in glee,
Making the stars giggle like bees!

Round and round the stars they spin,
To the rhythm of a cactus grin.
Galaxies break into fits of cheer,
In this cosmic party, let's persevere!

Who knew the void could be so bright?
With wobbly stars that dance at night.
So come and join this crazy spree,
In the laughter of the galaxy!

Lullabies of the Lonesome

Under a rock where the crickets serenade,
A chicken still dreams in a homemade glade.
With lullabies sung by frogs in a choir,
They pitch in with honks that never tire!

A moonbeam winks at the lonely snail,
Who wraps up in grass, telling its tale.
It whispers of dreams where it zooms and swirls,
Through fields of candy and whimsical worlds!

In a hammock made of spaghetti strands,
A bear reads stories with wiggly hands.
Each page is filled with jellybean lore,
As readers giggle, begging for more!

But wait! What's that in the sky?
A taco-shaped cloud, oh my, oh my!
It floats on by, just waving its cheese,
In this funny old world, there's never a freeze!

Musing in the Margins

On paper planes, the doodles fly,
While pencil wizards cast spells with a sigh.
A walrus wearing a tiny hat,
Waddles around like a dapper diplomat!

Through margins of books where oddities dwell,
Dancing numbers ring a jolly bell.
A pie chart dreaming of blueberry skies,
Plots a route where the laughter flies!

An octopus scribbles with eight wicked pens,
Writing notes that float to the ends.
Each note a giggle, a quirk, a pun,
Under the watchful eye of the sun!

Yet, the erasers get grumpy with fate,
Throwing tantrums, they contemplate.
But in the chaos, joy finds a home,
In the doodle-filled universe, we always roam!

Disturbances in the Depths

Bubbles pop in the depths so deep,
Where fish wear hats and never sleep.
A crab breaks into an awkward jig,
While seaweed sways, it starts to gig!

An octopus plays a tuba so grand,
With starfish clapping, a curious band.
They host a ball on the ocean floor,
Where laughter rings and creatures explore!

A whale in a bow tie joins with flair,
Adding melodies that float through the air.
Each note is a sprinkle of joy and delight,
As the manta rays twirl, bringing light!

But what's that bubbling up from below?
An angry clam puts on quite the show!
Yet even its fuss becomes a fun spree,
In the deep blue laughter, oh can't you see!

Cadences of the Clefted Heart

In a split of two, my heart did play,
Each half doing its own little ballet.
One sings loud, the other hums low,
Together they dance, though they steal the show.

Like a pair of socks, mismatched and bold,
Twirling in laughter, they break the mold.
One loves the rain, the other the sun,
In their silly battles, there's never a run.

With a giggle they gloat, oh what a sight,
Ping-ponging feelings day and night.
In confusion they thrive, in chaos they cheer,
What's only one story, becomes two, oh dear!

So here's to the halves, the quirky collide,
Finding joy in the gaps they can't hide.
Crazy together, they flutter and dart,
Cadences clash in the clefted heart.

Lyrics of the Liminal

Between the moments, the funny things dwell,
A whispering echo, a chuckling bell.
Time skips a beat, in a comical frame,
Turning the mundane into a game.

There's a dance in the air, a skip in the plot,
As shadows take jabs, jabbing smack with a thought.
A laugh from the liminal, it fills the abyss,
Every pause held hostage, in comedic bliss.

Chasing the footprints of memories missed,
Holding hands with awkward, clumsy twists.
In this peculiar gap, we find our delight,
As oddities serenade the shared night.

So prance in the awkward, in giggles we find,
Lyrics of whispers that swirl in the mind.
In the weirdness of life, joy always will bloom,
In the in-betweens, we dance and consume.

Visions Across the Void

Through the chasm we peek at the world outta sight,
With binoculars made of old cardboard white.
In the gaps, we guffaw at the silly parade,
Where bananas wear hats and cats try to wade.

We share jokes with echoes, as shadows do cheer,
In this empty space, laughter draws near.
Throwing paper airplanes with hopes tied with string,
Across the great void, silly banter we bring.

With a wink and a grin, we'll catch every fall,
Bouncing on laughs, we'll rise after all.
In the distance we see, our oddball delight,
A dance with the awkward, a comedy night.

To keep it all light, we send puns through the air,
Quaking in giggles, together we share.
With each silly vision, across we will glide,
Finding joy in the void, where folly's the guide.

Stanzas of Separation

From one side to another, with jest we divide,
In the absurdity of life, we take it in stride.
Half of me shouts, the other just winks,
As time pulls apart, oh how it blinks!

With a chuckle we ponder the things that we own,
In our mismatched slippers, we laugh at the known.
The socks do a tango, a one-legged spin,
In this quirky delight, where laughter begins.

A tickle of distance, a dainty pirouette,
In stanzas of separation, we mingle, not fret.
Waving a flag made of snacks, quite absurd,
Sharing whispered jokes, without a single word.

So we dance with the silly, through space and through time,
With giggles and hiccups, all caught in our rhyme.
In this lighthearted strife, we find what's divine,
In the gaps of existence, our laughter will shine.

Verses from the Vertigo

In a twirl and a spin, I lost my shoe,
Chasing a chicken, what else can I do?
Around and around, I went for a ride,
The laughter was loud, I could barely hide.

Upside-down world, where cats chase their tails,
Puppies in hats sail on wind-powered trails.
I slipped on a banana, oh dear, what a fuss,
Dancing with squirrels, just me and my bus.

Teetering teacups, they swirl in delight,
Balloons filled with giggles, they float out of sight.
I wrote a whole poem on a dizzying swing,
The laughter of children, oh, what joy they bring.

So here's to the topsy and the crazy we see,
In a world of endless fun, come spin here with me!

Harmonies in the Haze

In a foggy old park where ducks play the flute,
A frog in a top hat says, 'How cute is this brute?'
A kazoo plays the tunes as the llamas all prance,
While chickens in tutus prepare for a dance.

With noodles as microphones, pasta stars shine,
I'm serenaded by beans, they say, 'You're divine!'
The caterpillar croons with a voice so profound,
While the wise old owl nods, 'What a jam we've found!'

So let's hop on a cloud and float up high,
Where dwarves juggle moons while the fairies all fly.
With candy canes spinning, the world's a delight,
We'll sing through the haze, until morning's first light.

What fun it becomes when the oddballs unite,
With laughter and joy, we'll dance through the night!

Poems with Perilous Gaps

In a house made of gumdrops, the roof is a cake,
With candy cane pillars, all ready to shake.
I fell through a floor that was made out of pies,
And landed in jelly with wide-open eyes.

A squirrel in a cape flies with style and grace,
While turtles in tutus do the silliest race.
Balancing teacups, they wobbled and swayed,
With giggles erupting, they can't be delayed.

An octopus juggles spaghetti and cheese,
While laughing out loud, I fall down to my knees.
Finding my laughter in perilous spots,
In a whirlwind of fun, we forget all our thoughts.

So gather your pals, let's shout with great glee,
For the gaps that we face bring us joy, can't you see?

Threads of Tumult

In a whirlwind of yarn, the cats weave a tale,
While mice juggle buttons, all fit for a sail.
A circus of kittens performs pirouettes,
The audience cheers, filled with gasps and regrets.

With pies made of clouds; we twirl and we glide,
As flamingos with boots join the fun at our side.
A trumpet of hedgehogs plays tunes that go bop,
In this world of disorder, we'll never stop!

Dancing in spirals, we tumble and twist,
With laughter so loud, it's impossible to miss.
When chaos begins, let your spirits all soar,
For the threads of tumult bring joy evermore!

So join in the frolic, let the silliness spin,
In this tapestry of laughter, let's all count to ten!

Poetry of the Interstice

In a gap between the chairs,
A squirrel does the tango there.
With acorns as his twirly friends,
He spins and laughs as laughter trends.

A cactus tried to take a nap,
But woke up to a fluffy flap.
A pillow fights with cotton dreams,
While popcorn pops and squeaks and screams.

The shadows play with errant socks,
While teapots dance around in flocks.
The ticklish winds do cartwheels bright,
As giggles glide through morning light.

A wayward pencil scribbles lines,
In doodles, dragons strike up signs.
The kitchen sings with pots and pans,
In this odd realm of merry plans.

Whispers of a Wounded World

A banana peels a joke so sly,
While pigeons wear a bowtie high.
A turtle stumbles on a tune,
And joins a band with a froggy croon.

A cactus writes a heartfelt tale,
In the desert, laughter's never stale.
With sunflowers waltzing all around,
The world's a stage, a funny sound.

The clock ticks backward, what a sight!
The tea is cold, and soup takes flight.
A jellybean with thoughts to share,
Spreads giggles through the summer air.

With whispers of a world gone mad,
Even the grumpy cat is glad.
In every corner, chuckles brew,
As joy spills forth like morning dew.

Songs of the Shattered

A broken vase sings out of tune,
While laughing lamps sway with a swoon.
The table dances on three legs,
And offers tea from tiny kegs.

A mirror cracks to show a grin,
Reflecting all the chaos within.
As socks conspire to run away,
The fridge hums songs of yesterday.

The wallflowers whisper jokes at night,
While spoons debate who's wrong or right.
In laughter shared through glassy shards,
The world unfolds with whimsy cards.

Each broken piece, a tale to tell,
In awkwardness, we find our well.
The songs of all that seems askew,
Are symphonies of me and you.

Echoes of the Elusive

A wobbly chair squeaks out a rhyme,
While raccoons hold a coffee time.
Jellybeans plot to steal the show,
As cotton candy drifts with flow.

The echo giggles down the hall,
It tickles ears and makes us fall.
Whimsies dance in crinkled space,
While ricocheting jokes embrace.

A tangle of opposites align,
With lemons painted like a sign.
In fruitless tasks, the fun is found,
As laughter bounces all around.

The air is thick with playful puns,
And whispers sing like happy sons.
In elusive corners hid from view,
Echoes dance, unraveling true.

Serenade of the Split

In a field of giggles, I took a trip,
Where the grass was green, but slightly hip.
The cows wore shades, what a sight to see,
They danced and twirled, as carefree as me.

With a mirror pond that splashed in fun,
Two frogs sang duets, their work was done.
Jumping with glee, they stole the show,
While chasing flies with a comical flow.

Silly squirrels played tag on a branch,
Each leap and bound was a daring dance.
They wore tiny hats made from acorn tops,
And juggled berries until one plops.

Oh, the joy in this fractured land,
Where every moment seemed so unplanned.
Laughter erupted from every twist,
In this whimsical world that was hard to resist.

Poetic Parallels of the Plateaus

On a mountain high, two goats made a pact,
To bounce on the rocks with a comical act.
They leapt and they spun, then tumbled down,
Rolling and laughing, what a silly crown.

The clouds joined in with their fluffy style,
They tickled the goats, who giggled a mile.
With winds that whispered jokes through the air,
The peaks held secrets of laughter to share.

In valleys below, the flowers would sway,
Their petals would dance in a colorful play.
Each bloom had a joke, they'd shout it out loud,
A riot of colors, a giggling crowd.

So up in the sky, and down in the glades,
The fun never stopped, it danced like parades.
In poetic heights and down low in the folds,
The spirit of laughter a story unfolds.

Lyrics of the Lost

In a world of maps, I struck a deal,
To find the treasures that made me squeal.
But every path just led me to snacks,
With cookies and chips hiding in the cracks.

I asked a wise owl, with glasses so round,
"Where's the treasure?" I eagerly frowned.
He chuckled and scratched his bearded chin,
"Your loot is the laughter you find within!"

Then I tumbled into a whimsical maze,
With flickering signs that twisted my gaze.
All the lost lyrics sang in delight,
As I tried to dance under the soft moonlight.

And as I tripped over my own two feet,
I realized my journey was truly sweet.
No riches I found, just giggles and fun,
In a treasure of smiles that outshone the sun.

Melodic Mistrust

In a tavern loud, where shadows would play,
A cat sang songs that kept dogs at bay.
With a twitch of her tail and a wink in her eye,
She baffled the crowd, who laughed and sighed.

But the dog was clever, with tickets to spare,
He'd challenge the cat, a comedy affair.
With tunes that could bounce and rhythms that twist,
Their playful banter we just couldn't resist.

The audience cheered, for each clever jest,
As cat and dog battled, they gave it their best.
But who could declare who truly would win,
In a symphony matched with a feline's sly grin?

So let the music play, with a quirk and a twist,
And trust the laughter in the silly mist.
For when hearts are light, and the song's in the air,
Every note of mistrust just melts with a flare.

Fragments of the Fray

In a world of socks that never match,
I found a cat that loves to scratch.
With every tumble and silly fall,
We laugh till we can't breathe at all.

Bananas peel like slipping slides,
As we chase the dogs who love to hide.
The pie on the window, a tempting sight,
But it's more fun to take a bite!

The squirrels steal fruit with crafty glee,
While I dance around like a buzzing bee.
Finding humor in every little prance,
Life's a circus; join the dance!

With bubbles floating in a sunny breeze,
And lemonade spills that bring us to our knees,
In every fragment, laughter's the key,
Fractured fun, just you and me.

Landscapes of Longing

In gardens full of gnomes and cheer,
I long for snacks and a cold root beer.
The daisies giggle, the sunflowers sway,
As I try to nap but the bugs start to play.

The hammock swings, my dreams take flight,
But the cat decides it's time for a bite.
I chase after birds that dare to sing,
But trip on my shoelace: oh, what a fling!

The cake on the table calls my name,
But the frogs at the pond are playing a game.
Each leap and croak, a quirky tune,
While I ponder berries ripe in June.

In every landscape of silly sighs,
Laughter's the compass that never lies.
With a splash and a giggle, we wander around,
In every corner, joy is found.

Lines of Limitations

In a world where rules are meant to bend,
I tried to fly, but I fell off the mend.
With crayons dancing on the wall,
Our doodles proclaim, we're having a ball!

The kitchen's a mess, but what a delight,
As we bake cupcakes that take flight.
Flour fights and frosting wars,
Behind each disaster, laughter soars.

With rules like my socks, all mismatched and bright,
I twirl in the chaos, a curious sight.
Every tumble a lesson, every slip a cheer,
In the dance of limitations, we persevere.

So let's stack our worries and juggle our dreams,
In the whirl of existence, we burst at the seams.
With every line that tries to constrain,
We flip it around, then do it again!

Tapestry of the Torn

In a quilt made of crumbs and old pet hair,
We snuggle and giggle without a care.
With each stitch pulled tight, a tale to unfold,
Of mishaps and laughter, a tapestry bold.

The socks, they disappear, like magic they flee,
My left foot wonders, where can you be?
As mismatched pairs march on the floor,
I can't help but smile, who could ask for more?

With a seam ripped wide, and buttons to spare,
We craft silly hats and comb messy hair.
In every patchwork of woes and dreams,
We find humor in life's wild schemes.

So here's to the fabric of life we create,
With laughter and stories that never abate.
In a tapestry woven with joys ever torn,
We dance through the fibers, and new laughs are born.

Silences between the Stones

In a garden of gravel, minutes do sneak,
The stones start to chatter, oh what do they speak?
One says it's too quiet, another claims bold,
While a pebble insists it's just wanting pure gold.

A boulder rolls over, it gives quite a shrug,
'What's with all the silence? I'm feeling a bug!'
A shard of old history pipes up with a pun,
'Relax, my dear rock, life's just begun!'

In a patch of bright daisies, the giggles abound,
Rocks sharing their stories, not making a sound.
With a clatter and clink, they dance in the sun,
A party of pebbles, enjoying the fun.

So if you should wander where gravel does lay,
Listen closely, my friend, to what they would say.
For beneath all the silence, there's laughter so grand,
In the whispers of stones, life's wonders expand.

Sonnet of the Separation

Two socks in the dryer, oh what a mess,
One is bright red, the other a dress.
They tumble and twist, in a wild ballet,
Yet where is their partner? They've gone far away.

The dryer door squeaks, where do they go,
One sock says it's hot, but quite full of woe.
'If only we'd matched, what a sight we would make,
With patterns and colors, for goodness' sake!'

Yet one sock stays hopeful, while the other bemoans,
'You think there's a way to make it back home?'
They dream of the washers, their cycles in sync,
While sinking in suds, they sit back and think.

A spin and a tumble, they laugh and they sigh,
In the whirl of their fate, they find love can fly.
So onward they swirl, a duet not planned,
In the halls of the laundry, united they stand.

Threads of the Tangent

In a room made of threads and awkward handshakes,
A web of odd angles, with all of its quakes.
"I'm straight!" shouts a line, as it bends in a twist,
While a curve with a wink says, "You've got me missed!"

A circle rolls by, just a ball of pure fun,
"Why complicate life? Let's just roll in the sun!"
But the square pipes up, with its corners so neat,
"Tangents, my friends, make the world bittersweet."

As the angles collide, and the knots intertwine,
The threads all agree, it's quite hard to define.
With giggles and gaffes, they embrace all the bends,
In a tapestry woven, where humor transcends.

So if you feel stuck, in a point you can't flee,
Just remember the web, and the laughter it frees.
For every odd angle is a reason to cheer,
In the threads of the tangent, there's joy we hold dear.

Laments of the Liminal

In the doorway of dreams, where shadows do play,
A fellow stands asking, 'But where is my way?'
With a shrug of his shoulders, he sighs with a grin,
'Is this really living, or just where I've been?'

A ghost gives a chuckle, floats softly on air,
"Lament not my friend, there's magic to share!"
But the fellow just fidgets, his foot tapping fast,
"Tell me dear specter, is this moment my last?"

As the hourglass teeters, they ponder and twirl,
Fill the liminality with giggles and swirl.
'What if this ending is just a new start?'
With a wink from the ghost, they both play their part.

So leaping through liminal, a joke and a jest,
They paint with their laughter, a humorous quest.
For in every unknown, there's a punchline to find,
In the pauses of life, let the fun unwind.

Staggered Steps to Solitude

I tripped on a stone, my shoe took a leap,
The ground gave a laugh, as I started to creep.
A squirrel threw acorns, they danced with delight,
In my staggered steps, solitude takes flight.

I whispered my secrets to a shy little tree,
It chuckled and swayed, said, 'Come laugh with me!'
The bugs in the grass began a grand show,
As I staggered alone, they put on a glow.

My thoughts took a tumble, like leaves in a breeze,
The wind had a joke, it brought me to knees.
I chuckled in silence, a giggle so sweet,
In these silly steps, my heart found a beat.

So here in the quiet, my mind's a parade,
Dancing with shadows, no worries to trade.
With every odd stumble, I smile a bit wide,
In this weird little world, I gladly abide.

Chronicles of the Chasm

In a valley of echoes, my voice took a dive,
I shouted for help, but a goat came alive!
It bleated back tales of grand quests and dreams,
While I stood there wondering, or so it seems.

A bridge made of jellybeans, wobbled and swayed,
I dared take a step, then with laughter I played.
The chasm below giggled, 'What a sight to see!'
As I navigated candy with sheer jubilee.

My compass was spinning, a map made of snacks,
To follow its path, I just had to relax.
With chocolate chip routes and routes made of cheese,
Each step was a munch, I felt such a tease.

So here in this chasm, where whimsy does reign,
I scribble my stories, embrace the insane.
With every wild journey, a chuckle I find,
These chronicles echo, sweetly unlined.

Whispers Across the Divide

On a windy cliffside, I turned to the breeze,
It tickled my ear and whispered with ease.
'There's a dance in the shadows, a giggle to share,
Where the hills roll like laughter, beyond any care.'

A rabbit hopped by, wearing spectacles bright,
He winked and he nodded, said, 'Oh, what a sight!'
We shared our odd thoughts as the sun took a dip,
Across this great divide, on a whimsical trip.

I tossed him a carrot, he tossed back a pun,
Together we plotted a voyage for fun.
With whispers like secrets from valleys so wide,
Each chuckle resounded, with joy as our guide.

The stars above twinkled, a spark in each beam,
They winked at the dark, as if catching a dream.
Though divided by distance, we found common ground,
In laughter and whispers, true friendship was found.

Echoes of Distant Shores

The ocean was chatty, with waves playing tricks,
I danced with the sand, while seagulls did flicks.
It called out my name in a splash and a whoosh,
As I skipped with the tide, feeling eager to swoosh.

A crab gave a nod, wore a hat made of grass,
He scuttled in rhythm, as if full of sass.
I laughed at its antics, a show to behold,
The echoes of fun, in the waves, they unfold.

With every soft whisper, the breeze whispered tales,
Of fish that wore bowties, and whales riding snails.
I clapped like a child, so caught in the moment,
While the sea shared its stories, like sweet, salty condiment.

So here by the shore, where the silly abound,
In echoes of laughter, my joy knows no bound.
Each splash is a chuckle, each tide a reprise,
In the dance of the ocean, I find my own prize.

Verses Through the Veil

There once was a ghost who played tricks,
He hid all the socks with his flicks.
The laundry would dance,
In a mischievous prance,
As the ghost laughed and turned into bricks.

A witch brewed a potion quite wild,
With a frog who refused to be mild.
He jumped in her stew,
And out he just flew,
Proclaiming, 'I'm no longer beguiled!'

The ghouls in the graveyard would sing,
While bats on the swing took a fling.
They squeaked such a tune,
Under the bright moon,
Making nighttime a humorous thing.

So should you creep close to the night,
Don't fear, for they're not here to fright.
Just giggles and glee,
As they dance wild and free,
In this odd, silly world of delight.

Textures of the Teardrop

A teardrop decided to roll,
With a bump and a giggle, oh soul!
It splashed on the floor,
And begged for some more,
To join in the laughter, that's whole.

In puddles of joy they would play,
Reflecting the world in their sway.
They painted a scene,
With colors so keen,
Making all the sad feelings stray.

A raindrop claimed, 'I am not shy!',
As it danced with a leap to the sky.
'I'll tickle your cheeks,
With my playful peaks,
And bring forth a grin, oh my, oh my!'

So gather your tears, if you have,
And let them all dance in a cab.
For laughter's the goal,
To lighten the soul,
In the textures of joy that we nab.

Threads of Tension

A spider spun webs with a twist,
Making sure no bugs went amiss.
With a flick of her leg,
She gave each a beg,
'Stay still, or you'll end up dismissed!'

The webs caught a breeze, what a scene!
They danced like they wore a costume queen.
But with each tangled thread,
Came a giggle instead,
As the flies made their grand in-between.

The ants held a meeting of sorts,
To measure the lengths of their shorts.
They laughed at the sizes,
In their tiny disguises,
While debating their summertime sports.

In the garden where chaos collides,
The bugs have their joyful rides.
So join in the fun,
When the day is done,
And see where the laughter abides.

Liminal Echoes

In a place where shadows do play,
There's a creature who loves to delay.
With a wink and a grin,
He pulls you right in,
While the sun goes to hide for the day.

He whispers sweet tales of the air,
And jokes about things that aren't there.
With a flick of his tail,
He tells each grand tale,
Of a world full of laughter and flair.

A cat claims the dusk brings a dance,
And drags all the mice in a trance.
With a flick of his ear,
He draws them all near,
For a midnight frolic, not chance.

So linger in this playful space,
Where sounds of hilarity grace.
In echoes of light,
In the midst of the night,
Join the fun in this whimsical place.

Melodies in the Void

A chicken danced on a cloudy beam,
Flapping wings like a kooky dream.
It tripped on air, then jumped in glee,
  Singing tunes for the bumblebee.

A squirrel laughed at the silly sight,
Wearing shades, oh what a delight!
It grabbed a nut and did a spin,
Declaring victory with a cheeky grin.

Around them swirled the cosmic dust,
  Adding sparkle to each little gust.
A cat joined in with a comedic pounce,
Making all the laughter really bounce.

In this void where fun will reign,
The wacky antics never wane.
So grab a friend, let loose and play,
  In this space where giggles stay.

Fractured Footsteps

A penguin waddled with flair and pride,
Slipped on ice, what a wild ride!
It flopped and flailed with a flurry of feet,
Creating a dance, oh what a treat!

A moose chuckled from a snowy knoll,
Watching the penguin lose control.
It stomped its hooves in a rhythmic way,
Joining the fun, hip-hop ballet!

Then out jumped a goat, full of mirth,
With a jig that gripped the frozen earth.
Foam on its beard, it pranced around,
Making sure that joy was found!

In fractured footsteps, they swayed and spun,
Bounding about, oh what fun!
The laughter echoed, bright as the moon,
In this snowy dance, we sing a tune.

Cadences of the Canyon

A parrot squawked on a canyon wall,
Echoing tales of a fumbled fall.
It flapped in rhythm with a playful flair,
As rabbits giggled and danced in the air.

A lizard slid with a slippery cheer,
Sass in its tone, not a hint of fear.
It leaped on a rock with an oversized grin,
Challenging shadows to come jump in!

The river chuckled, whispering low,
Adding beats to the chaos below.
Fish leaped up, catching the show,
Joining in on the canyon's throw!

In this place where jesters unite,
Every giggle is pure delight.
So let the world hear this joyful sound,
In the canyons where fun's always found!

Verses from the Vortex

A whirlpool spun with a silly twist,
Where rubber ducks played, none could resist.
They quacked in harmony, such a loud cheer,
As they slid down a funnel, full of good cheer.

A walrus waved with a goofy grin,
Scaling the circling water's din.
It launched into the swirl with panache,
Landing with grace, oh what a splash!

A fish in shades did the funky flow,
With moves too wild, stealing the show.
They whirled and twirled in a vibrant spree,
Using the vortex to set spirits free!

In this swirl of jests and jesters,
Laughter and fun are the true investors.
So grab a friend; come dance and dive,
In the vortex where joy comes alive!

Musings of the Misplaced

In the land of socks and lonely shoes,
A chicken dances, singing the blues.
The banjo plays with a squeaky beat,
While ants march around, tapping their feet.

A cat in pajamas, looking quite grand,
Tells jokes to a cactus, who's too stiff to stand.
The moon peeks in with a curious grin,
As fish on bicycles spin round and spin.

A fridge hums softly, the cables all crossed,
While veggies debate if they've been tossed.
A pickle winks at a loaf of bread,
In this bumpy world, no one's mislead.

Laughter erupts from the toaster and tea,
Dancing through life, so carefree and free.
In this strange place where oddities roam,
Even the furniture feels right at home.

Cadences of the Chasm

A squirrel with shades, so snazzy and cool,
Flips through the air, breaking all of the rules.
With a flip and a flop, he lands with a grin,
As the grass starts to giggle, pulling him in.

A frog wearing glasses croaks out a song,
In a voice quite jazzed, a little off throng.
He sways by the lily with flair and with style,
While dragonflies spin and twirl for a while.

The clouds hold a picnic, with rainbows on plates,
As the sun tells the stories of all of life's fates.
With laughter ricocheting, the breezes all hum,
Who knew that the chasm could be so much fun?

Now gather the critters, the party's begun,
With walruses breakdancing, oh what a run!
In this mighty chasm where joy takes the lead,
The oddest of moments plants the best seed.

Whispers of the Wilderness

In the wild woods where the mushrooms wear hats,
The rabbits hold meetings with political bats.
They debate about carrots and who'll get the fries,
As the owls look over with wise, sleepy eyes.

A tree trunk is singing, quite out of tune,
While squirrels throw nuts at a crescent moon.
The berries all giggle, a ripe, rosy hue,
As trees share their gossip and dance with the dew.

The wind plays the flute with a tickle and tease,
While the bushes play tag with the buzzing of bees.
A raccoon in glasses, with papers to sort,
Is busy researching the fine art of sport.

Oh, the wilderness whispers with quirks and delight,
In the dance of the day and the spotlight of night.
Where laughter echoes and nonsense takes flight,
A world full of joy, forever in sight.

Echoic Expressions

A parrot with bling squawks riddles so bright,
As a turtle in shades takes a wild, slow flight.
The meadow's alive with a jubilant shout,
While the daisies all dance, letting loose without doubt.

An echo of giggles rolls over the hill,
Bouncing off boulders, producing health spills.
The grasshoppers jump, sharing tales from the sky,
As the butterflies flutter, oh my, oh my!

A walrus on stilts tries to balance with flair,
While beavers are busy with watertight care.
They laugh at the moonbeam that tickles the pond,
Transforming reflections, a world so far beyond.

With laughter resounding, the echoes replay,
As the night leans in to join in the fray.
In this grand symphony, each voice finds their choice,
Together their antics rejoice in one voice.

Eclipsed Expressions

In shadows where the giggles hide,
A cat in a hat takes a wild ride.
With shoes on his paws, he dances round,
In a world where silly knows no bound.

The moon trips over a cheese-like hill,
While squirrels in suits dash with a thrill.
A banana peels laughter from the trees,
As tittering whispers flutter with ease.

Pigs wearing wigs twirl in delight,
Chasing their tails under starlight bright.
With every turn, the laughter spills,
In a festival where the whimsy thrills.

So let the giggles twine and dance,
In a game of jest, not a single chance.
They spin and they whirl, all in good cheer,
An expression eclipsed, yet crystal clear.

Ballads of the Breach

A bear on a unicycle rolls by,
Juggling some pies that fly high.
Majestic and silly, he takes a bow,
Inviting the giggles, come one, come all!

The birds in the trees wear tiny hats,
Singing loud songs while dodging the rats.
With flapping wings and a dance so bright,
They choreograph chaos from morning to night.

A frog in a tux jumps on a stage,
Reciting bad puns, unleashing his rage.
The crowd rolls with laughter, oh what a sight,
In ballads of breach, where jesters take flight.

With melodies swirling like leaves in the air,
The world spins around with its whimsical flair.
Each note an adventure, each laugh a delight,
In the grandest of concerts, where humor takes flight.

Reflections in the Rift

A fish on a skateboard looks so amazed,
Gliding through puddles in a watery haze.
It flips and it flops, then takes a quick spin,
As laughter erupts from the folks gathered in.

In mirrors of whimsy, the waves ripple fast,
Where jokes float like bubbles, dangling and cast.
A crab in a bowtie declares it quite grand,
With a shimmy and shake, he steals the cool stand.

The clouds above giggle, puffing away,
Sprinkling rainbows to lighten the day.
With reflections of humor, it's a splashy delight,
In a rift full of jest that ignites endless light.

So gather the chuckles and let them resound,
For in this joyous glitch, we are humor-bound.
With every reflection, the fun multiplies,
In the rippling echoes where laughter relies.

Lyrical Landscapes of Loss

In fields where the daisies wear frowns on their heads,
The wind carries whispers of funnies unsaid.
A turtle in glasses reads jokes with a grin,
While butterflies chuckle, they just can't help in.

An elephant trips on a vine laced with cheer,
Landing in puddles that gleam crystal clear.
Each splash echoes laughter, though things seem quite grim,
For even in loss, the humor won't dim.

A squirrel with a scowl climbs up an old tree,
Complaining the world is just too wobbly.
But look! There's a raccoon in a marigold dress,
Dancing away, who can't help but impress!

So next time you wander through lands tinged with gloom,
Remember the joy that laughter can bloom.
In landscapes of loss, find the giggles and grace,
For the heart loves to smile, even in the oddest place!

Poetics of the Parted

When socks get lost in the dryer's spin,
Each one alone, a life full of sin.
They tell their tales of daring escapes,
With wild adventures and silly shapes.

A sandwich once fell on the floor with a thud,
It dreamed of a life where it sailed the flood.
But gravity won, and now it's just spread,
Cursing the hands that wished it was fed.

Two spoons engaged in a heated debate,
Arguing loudly over who's really great.
One claimed it stirrer was far more refined,
While the other just laughed at the mess it designed.

A cat in a tree with a look full of sass,
Declared, "I'm an eagle! Just give me some grass!"
But the ground disagreed and the owners just sighed,
"Please come down, dear feline, it's time to decide!"

Sonnet of the Silent

There's wisdom found in the quietest pens,
Whispering truths where the noise never ends.
A pencil once thought it could speak out loud,
But found its voice lost in a recalcitrant crowd.

An umbrella once opened for a grand dance,
Tripped its own self, and lost all its chance.
It now sits alone, feeling rather blue,
Wishing for rain and a partner or two.

The toaster burned bread that had lofty dreams,
Now it only dreams of the toast and the creams.
In its metallic heart, a wish hangs quite low,
To rise from the ash and put on a show.

The fridge hums softly a tune of regret,
Telling of snacks that we stubbornly let,
Go stale and forgotten, in darkness they lurch,
While broccoli echoes, "I needed a church!"

Resonant Refrains

A rubber duck floats with a wise little grin,
It quacks out the secrets of bath time's din.
While soap bubbles dance in a frothy ballet,
They giggle and pop, inviting the play.

The microwave beeps with enthusiasm bright,
"Dinner's done now! Come back for a bite!"
But everyone's gone, relics of time's race,
And it ponders its life in this empty space.

The clock on the wall is a mischievous thief,
Stealing our moments, revealing no grief.
It jingles and chimes like a playful old friend,
Yet, always reminds that all good things end.

A carpet, once pristine, now shows its wear,
It tells of feet dancing and the joy in the air.
With stains and stories that decorate its face,
It laughs at the chaos, delighting in grace.

Chronicles of the Chasm

A gopher once waved from a hole in the ground,
Shouting, "Hey there! Have you seen my mound?"
His friends all looked down and teased from above,
"Don't dig too deep; you'll lose all your love!"

Two mushrooms debated who grew up the best,
One claimed it was humor, the other, a jest.
They sprouted all tall with caps held so high,
But tripped on their roots, both fell with a sigh.

The fence post stood proud, a sentry aloof,
Guarding complaints from the roof to the roof.
It listened intently, then said with a laugh,
"Life's better with humor, let's seal it with craft!"

A squirrel and crow had a contest of speed,
Racing through branches to fulfill a need.
With acorns for prizes and chips in the air,
They learned that some laughter beats running with flair.

www.ingramcontent.com/pod-product-compliance
Lightning Source LLC
Chambersburg PA
CBHW051639160426
43209CB00004B/713